in the fire

dayna gosselin

in the fire © 2018 by Dayna Gosselin
All rights reserved. No element of this book may be reproduced in any form without direct permission from the author.

@daynagosselinwriting

ISBN-13: 978-1775222613

*you slice through
my thick skin
unleashing my passion
to bleed
poetry*

trigger warning

the content beyond this page may contain triggering and/or explicit content

topics such as
mental health
abuse
trauma
sexual innuendo
are explored

please seek assistance if needed

contents

in the heat 9

in the flames 21

out of the ashes 89

into the clouds 125

becoming water 151

in the
heat

in the fire

it was a combination
of sun and rain
to keep our spark
alive and dying
all at once

turn off the lights
hold a match
between your fingers
and gently flick
to ignite the passion
you'll notice
the best kind of interaction
is when heat rises
with love

in the fire

stir together
lay on the baking sheet
heat the oven
pour in the cream

we're making love

dayna gosselin

you hold onto the arms of the chair
leaning back
to relax
but every time you get off
you're exhausted

in the fire

my body temperature rises
when you kiss me
my cheeks burn from the intensity
as you grip me
tonight
we find love
tomorrow
we find the cold shoulder
where the burn feels the same
but it's frost bite
where i still scream your name
just *different* than last night

it's fire *then* ice

dayna gosselin

one day it's scars you beg for
on your back
from fingernails
late at night
another day it's scars you beg for
them to stop
giving you
with their knife

-a lover's back stab

in the fire

our bodies are made of water
yet we still found a way
to burn one
another

dayna gosselin

you let the butterflies blister inside me
until they were left without wings
unable to fly away from you
like a caterpillar crawling back
even when
i didn't want to

in the fire

you remind me of tea
the way it warms my body
soothes my soul
hot underneath
my fingertips
and when it touches my lips
all i taste is you
but i'm afraid to
call it my favorite drink
because when you leave
i know i'll never feel *relief*
again

we appeared to no longer be allies
i tried to flee the battle scene
to retreat out the front door
instead of fighting until victory

i remember not wanting any more
innocent blood
to be shed
but you stood in the doorway
refusing to let me leave
without a fight

you forced me
to use the sharpness of my words
to pierce you
into your already bleeding heart
then pled
for me to spare your life

but i showed no mercy
to the casualty who entered war
without proper artillery

you should have known
i'd rather lose you
than a battle

-a stubborn war

in the
flames

in the fire

all it takes
is one match
to burn you

-relationships

dayna gosselin

we are all stars
constantly struggling against the force
of our own gravity
trying not to collapse or
burnout

in the fire

it's the fire within
that can spread
unapologetically
anger
jealousy
the flames of humanity
we try to contain
with each breath
but we are dragons
quenched by fire
to fill our empty
parts

dayna gosselin

rounding my sharp edges
altered my shape
i didn't need to change
only someone to embrace
me at my roughest

in the fire

you disappear with the horizon
as the darkness creeps in
you're not as beautiful
as a sun setting
and you only seem to rise
as the light starts appearing

i need someone who stays
in between my sunset
and sunrise

someone who isn't afraid
of my darkness

dayna gosselin

they come into your life
as graciously as a waterfall
everything seems to flow
until they crash you
into the rocks
below

that's what happens
with *rushing*
water

if they stand over you
making you feel insignificant and small
they're not worthy of your love

if they beg on their knees
and you start to feel like they
are

remember
a change in height
doesn't change their heart

dayna gosselin

we all make
mistakes
but if you make multiple
the same way
and never calculate
what it can equal
you can count me out
because leaving isn't rocket science
it's simple math

in the fire

trace your scars back to the knife
that sliced you into pieces
as a requiem
for all the reasons
to stay away

why do you always leave
the door open for them
and continue to say
welcome
as they step
all over you

you are not a doormat
you are human

did you forget
again

in the fire

you give me one reason to stay
that outweighs
a thousand reasons
to leave
there is no balance
when our insecurities
weigh the heaviest

within our silence
i still scream for you
to stay
don't let my stubborn act
fool you
into thinking
i'll be okay without you

because i'm not

in the fire

it hurts to breathe
all i seem
to do is inhale
every memory and thought of you
am i the prison
refusing to release you
to let you go
or am i the prisoner
with a life sentence
forced to reform
and exhale

dayna gosselin

unspoken words hang in the air
like clouds of ash
choking
in this state of limbo

in the fire

the truth is
lies can be soft
like their lips
to cradle you
from the rough edges
of their teeth

neither of our hands
could remain clean
from all the dirt we brought up
on one another
when we were
angry

-buried ourselves again

in the fire

when there's a rupture
in our crust
we rumble with anger
bleeding onto
everything and everyone
in the way

we are volcanoes
spewing lava
instead of love

dayna gosselin

you are not broken
you don't need repairs
so why let them weld you
into something else

in the fire

my house is empty
with walls missing pictures
of our memories
replaced with beautiful
decorations
picked up from the bar
but somehow
outside beauty
still can't make this abandoned house
look tempting
no one asks to reside anymore
one walk through on all the floors
then they leave
the neighbors say i'm run down now
not as vibrant and put together
i hear them whisper
through the windows of my mind
but i never learned how
to rebuild myself
i relied on you to fix me

i'm bathing in our memories
trying to drown every thought of you
i didn't understand
when i tried to wash you away
my skin begged me to stop
they call it first love
but i call it
bad luck

-contaminated

in the fire

i've been called every name
in the book
but the most offensive name
you called me was
hers

dayna gosselin

when they sprinkle love
you act as if their sweetness
can complete you
but a sundae is still a sundae
without the extras
on top

in the fire

when a heart breaks
it acts like a broken compass
pointing in the wrong direction
thinking it needs someone else's mending
instead of its own
love and affection

dayna gosselin

do not ask me why
when you answer
with your actions
why i left

in the fire

stop giving
rope to those
who don't want to
climb out

-chances

time stood still
everyone moved on
except me
maybe i was the one
standing
forgetting to move
my feet
as the clock
continued to click
all around me

we spend time
as if it comes cheap
like we can purchase it
after it's used
but the jobs we work
for money
can't buy more for
friends and family
goals and dreams
i would give anything
to get it back
for something we already get
for free

it's too expensive to waste

dayna gosselin

kindness
cannot quench a thirst
for fire

why do our teeth sharpen at the thought
of an apology
why do our tongues find a way out
beyond their cage
why do words enter into the world
in anger
only leaving us with a bitter taste
how do we not see that
revenge
is not so sweet
it is sour and fiery
spoiling every taste bud
we have
where any flavor we get
is just pure
emptiness

dayna gosselin

we live on a spectrum
hurting and healing
ourselves and others
taking and giving
never really remaining
on one side
because humanity has more
than just two faces

in the fire

let's blow bubbles again
like kids
living in bliss
laughing as we pop them
over our heads
let's be kids again
instead of adults
i'm tired of being angry
when someone bursts
ours

dayna gosselin

we wish upon stars
far away
and forget to
appreciate
the light within reach

-jealousy

in the fire

love birds
fall from the nest
when their wings
aren't ready

-flying solo

dayna gosselin

caged by a white picket fence
with perfect flowers
dreaming of another life
where the wood is rotting
and the grass isn't quite as green
because happiness still seems
to grow over there

in the fire

people are not
pit stops
to get what you want
so you can hit the road
again
until you see the next
turn off

do you have a
final destination
or is the drive
to keep on moving

-road trip

dayna gosselin

you were a safe bet
but i wanted to risk everything
to feel what it was like
to be in the arms of danger
maybe then i wouldn't feel
like i was losing
out

-love is a gamble

in the fire

a word
of different origins
defined and translated
by experience

is your definition
feeling right or wrong
for what we deem is
love

dayna gosselin

they say
people look their best
when wearing red
exquisite
powerful
ready to take *on* the world
but have they seen
when people put on their face
the same color
angry
powerful
ready to take *over* the world

it's a deadly look

in the fire

we lend our heart
to borrow theirs
but not all hearts
can be returned

-library

dayna gosselin

loneliness
does not have boundaries
it sneaks into
your covers at night
even when you're in bed
with someone else

in the fire

if they stop
crying a river
it does not mean
they're no longer
drowning

dayna gosselin

they are afraid
to leave
so they stay
why is the fear of loss
stronger than
the hope to gain

in the fire

you cut me open like a surgeon
tear my heart from my chest
with no intent
to fix the broken parts
yet
it won't stop beating
for you

dayna gosselin

i made you the landlord
of my heart
but you only wanted
to be a tenant

-rented

built you a home in every city
but you still wanted the girl next door

-neighbors

they ask for distance
and you hang onto a string
of hope
wasting beneath your fingers
as they slowly
pull further away
until you finally let go

-a kite lost in a windstorm

in the fire

weeping for days
bags form under my eyes
carrying pain
with your photograph
in hands that once
held you the same

i saw your face
one more time
wearing a smile
next to mine

it truly was
a sight for sore eyes

dayna gosselin

searching every channel
on the radio
for a song that won't
remind me of you
but even white noise
sings about your absence

in the fire

my heart called for you
but we were disconnected
by differences
how am i still hung up
when you're out of range

-some nights it only took one bar for you to be in service

one day you will hear my name again
you will know the title of every book i write
looking for a way to read my words
with your wife
in the next room
to see if i admit
i miss you
but the more you read
the more you'll be confused
because today
i do
but tomorrow
has yet to come

and i write every night

in the fire

photographs tell me you're happy
but we both know they lie

like ours did

if you think
remaining on the shelf
is the worst thing
then you've never been
read
as a bedtime story
borrowed and returned
to a library of men
providing reviews
you never asked for

no

if you think
remaining on the shelf
is the worst thing
then you've never been
reused

in the fire

i am not bare
when you strip me
i am clothed
with regret

dayna gosselin

if they search for depth
underneath your clothes

they're shallow

each hand draws differently
so every line will never look
the same
but we need to respect
their way
so never cross anyone's line
without a personal invite

-boundaries

i'm not a bike to ride for leisure
i don't wheel around
like you
looking for straight and narrow roads
avoiding bumps and windings
in the path to a body
holding onto someone's sides
like handle bars
trying to steer them into
who they should be
i'm not a bike with handle bars
i'm a human with love handles
waiting to be held
the way i deserve

in the fire

tried to drown you out
with tears
but all you do
is swim through my head

dayna gosselin

nothing feels set in stone
until you see them
not alone
anymore

you couldn't take me as i am
so i knew
i was too strong
for you
to take me straight
when the chase
ran out

-a toast to the end of us

if you stumble across my words
years later
and your heart falls
at the thought of my fingers still creating
magic
even after our spark burned
out
maybe your new love will catch you
because i am not your safety net
anymore
i am not going to pick you up
at 2 am
after six drinks and another mistake
i am the one who will give you
your wake up call
the next the morning
when you look down
and see cheap lipstick
against your skin
i never wore

in the fire

parched lips surrounding
a sandy desert tongue
craving just
one more sip
is it
just a mirage
or have i really not
had you for
this long

-dry spell

dayna gosselin

tears blur our memory
decisions haunt like a ghost
from love to enemy
how i miss you the most

racing thoughts replaced your voice
sleep hides my waking sorrow
from yesterday to today's choice
how i wish today was tomorrow

hung over or hung up
both hurt the same
the next day

dayna gosselin

do you use love
or make it
you can't do both

in the fire

tore my own flesh
just to reflect
the pain killed me
to look inside
and bring myself
back to life

out of
the ashes

in the fire

i envy the way ashes
dance in the sun
after a forest fire

the flame
did not burn
their zest for life

dayna gosselin

fire swallows us whole
until we blister in a pit
of agony
a party invite
exclusive to demons
nailing every angel
to a post we cannot abandon
we must watch
as the flames scorch every part of us
until we crumble
to notice the good in us
can still rise
within the ruins of life

in the fire

at the bottom
i found the rocks
to build a stronger
empire

and the foundation
to expand
my mind

hitting
rock bottom
helped me rise

dayna gosselin

it may seem like your world
is falling apart
where pieces seem out of place
as you try to fit them back
together
but do not let it puzzle your mind
the world changes
and so will you

it will all fit together
again

in the fire

we harbor mistakes
on the shore of our mind
where the tide
cannot wash away
these anchored lessons

dayna gosselin

it is
your own flesh
that keeps you together
your own bones
that always support you
it is
the way you are built
strong and sturdy
so don't let anything
sweep you away from the truth
or off your feet

in the fire

we stand in cross fire
where every shot they take
can knock us down
but we need to step out of the flame
to rebuild and regain
ourselves

dayna gosselin

do not accept
the hurt
forgive
to soothe the pain

in the fire

open the windows
to air out your mind
rest your worries
close your eyes
let the wind blow
the pain aside
there is no better time
than now
to let it go

dayna gosselin

we fall with
change
and decompose like a leaf
then bring ourselves back
into the world
in a new form

it's the cycle of life

in the fire

she's different now
the stars in her eyes
turned into galaxies
with endless possibility

there are no boundaries

cut ties with those holding you down
they will keep you there
for as long as they can

do not be afraid when their grasp tightens
it is only from the rope slipping away
from their hands
and
do not be afraid to release yourself
you deserve to rise above

you will find
after all this time
you weren't really tied to anyone
or anything
except yourself

in the fire

tighten your self worth
don't let it fray
as you climb away
from rock bottom

-tight rope

dayna gosselin

within all the tears
there isn't a silver lining
there is a colorful discovery

in the fire

lessons from a candle

without the burn
you wouldn't be
as bright

dayna gosselin

it's in our roots
to grow from tears
that water our worries
to grow from laughter
that lights our life
we can only blossom
from a combination
of weather

and today we will grow
rain or shine

in the fire

let the current take you
far from the shore of safety
let the waves crash over your body
and push you aside
when the tide changes
let it shape you into a beautiful rock
a combination of sharp and soft
someone will find
and cherish

arising from the cracks of a volcano
that once erupted
are ashes
now floating across the sky
making friends with the sun
an act of compassion
after burning
relentlessly

and you can too

in the fire

be as gentle on your wounds
as you are
with theirs

dayna gosselin

clean slate

when we bring out
our dirty laundry
it's time to change
the cycle

in the fire

promise me
you will never
lose yourself or
stop loving yourself
even if
you love and lost
them

the weight of the word
is heavy
it continues to be
carried and passed around
let it go
drop the burden
feel light enough to
float towards the sun
away from the storm
because
blame
should not be caged
it needs to be
released and undone

in the fire

miracles do not happen
when hearts are closed
they happen when you feel
all the amazing things
life can bring
big and small

-clarity

dayna gosselin

i remained true to myself
so when you threatened to
expose me
for who i wasn't
i stood there
completely naked
and smiled

in the fire

today
be who you want to be
because tomorrow
is never guaranteed
wouldn't you rather be *happy*
for your last day on earth

dayna gosselin

change rips us
from our safety net
lets us fall face first
into the hard ground
where the bottom
lets us choose to
stand again
or make friends
with the rocks

in the fire

once she no longer feared
the art of letting go
she was able to
paint the most beautiful
picture of life
with everything she still
had

dayna gosselin

you tried to strip me
of who i am
but you forgot
i am born
naked

in the fire

i am bare
exposed completely
no longer
who others want me to be

i am bare
not willing dress myself
to shelter you from who i am
because of the acceptance you lack
for your bones
on your back

i am bare
releasing myself from the skin
that imprisons me
from societal views
that consumes those
who refuse
to be free

i am bare
exposed completely
to my bones

and i am strong when
stripped
naked
and
exposed

when events and people
throw stones
to break you
let the ripple effect of agitation
flow without consequence
this is your *becoming* of water
this is your *cleansing* of fire

in the fire

we each have our turn
to either
continue to burn
those who burn us
or become the water
that puts hate
to rest

-in the fire

dayna gosselin

sometimes two trees
need to grow
in different fields
even though their roots
will always be
connected

it's okay to grow apart

how to keep passion alive

when the spark starts to burn out
find wood
or find a new
match

into the clouds

i never liked the relationship question
can i do better
no one is less than
or above you
instead ask yourself
is there someone better suited
for me

-oranges and apples

dayna gosselin

when i felt blank
and empty inside
you handed me a book
of inspiration
my ink changed from craving
words of pain
to writing about the one
who gave me rhythm

-meaningful lines

it wasn't love at first sight
it was intrigue
the kind of curiosity
that lasts

a lifetime

dayna gosselin

we dance in moonlight
with hands intertwined
whispering lullabies
to the stars
thanking the world
for tangling our beautiful souls
in darkness

in the fire

heating from the core of our
existence
we fuse together
creating energy to light
up the world
when clouds try to get in
our way
we continue to rise above
because it's
love
the sun that keeps us all
from dying

dayna gosselin

i am not an empty field
to plant your seeds
i am the forest
you can water
to help me
grow

i am myself with
or without you

in the fire

my heart
is already so full of love
it cannot be filled by you
but it always has room
to grow

it's a healthy stretch

to the one
who truly looks for
depth
underneath my skin
not just my clothes
you're the only one
who can uncover
my soul

attention can blind
a troubled
heart

find someone
who loves
with their eyes shut

you're ordinary
with an extra twist
i always wished
to tangle my soul
in extraordinary ways

bouncing ideas off one another
we're able to jump higher
reaching our dreams and goals
that once seemed too distant
like a trampoline
i bounce you
and you bounce me

-double jump

dayna gosselin

i love when i'm in
the heat of summer
and when i'm not
your warmth
to defrost
my winter

in the fire

sandy toes
walking along the shore
rays of sunshine
on my face
the other in my hand
darling i'm on vacation
whenever i'm with you

-sunny days

dayna gosselin

we can furnish any empty room
in our hearts
with love

-we are all interior decorators

you host them for years
in your heart
until one day
they ask
if they can be more
than just a guest

will you say yes

dayna gosselin

not another fish in the sea
i am the whole body
of water
shallow and deep
calm and rough
if you dare to jump inside
be certain you can swim
through every tide
change

in a sea of sentences
flowing from anger
water rushes over my rock
he's pushed to the edge
yet standing his ground
he's immovable
when i am not

-grounded by love

my heart like a compass
pointed north towards a place that did not exist
on any map

the crew told me it was broken
the water ahead looked rough
unlike the south
which looked like smooth sailing

it had to be broken
but what if it wasn't
i thought
they laughed then left

i knew sailing into the unknown would be a risk
especially alone
but my ship was built for exploration
so was the captain

the next day i set sail for the north

and that's where i found you sailing into the south
exploring the unknown alone
because your compass pointed
in that direction

we laughed then smiled

now we knew that the water was no different in the
north or south
it was our perception of the unknown

in the fire

that skewed the way we viewed the sea
that's when i knew my heart would never change its course
it belonged in the north

it belonged with you

recite me
like your favorite poem
take me
on a journey of emotion
give me
one title to state your devotion

say i'm yours

in the fire

your kiss
tastes so sweet
how did the last person
not like candy

dayna gosselin

the walls you see
were built by the person
before you
who tried to fix them

don't bulldoze it down

wait for them
to build you a door
and let you in

*if you're patient
kind and understanding*
their heart can open up
again

in the fire

anyone can acclimatize
their cold ways
by insulating their hearts
with love

becoming
water

build within your ashes

in the fire empowers readers to build within their ashes after becoming burnt out from different types of relationships.

Through four distinct chapters, readers embark on a journey through passion – healthy and unhealthy. During this journey, readers are able to discover their ability to decide their own path: to either continue the flame, burning their self and others, or to rebuild from their ashes and become water.

Becoming water is a choice everyone can make to put out pain. It's easy to want to burn those who burned us. But hate spreads like a forest fire until nothing aside from pain remains. We all have the ability to stop it with love and kindness.

What will you become?

-becoming water after burning in the fire

my burnt flesh is peeling
my thin layer of skin crumbles
exposing my raw self
now layered with thicker skin
it is not flesh that is burning
it is the flame inside me
ready to immerse from the ashes

One day I woke up in flames. The world I knew was crumbling to the ground. I was burning and the pain was unbearable. I ran to my friend's house screaming, accidently spreading the fire. We both burned that night. On the way home, a stranger lent me their hand and tucked me into bed. The next morning, I woke up in ashes. Burnt out, I knew I had to change something. So I rebuilt myself from the ground up. With thicker skin that could resist fire and a garden hose for arms, I ran back to my friend's house. There, I lent my hand and water poured out.

-the author's choice to become water

if you're burned
tend to your wounds
soothe your skin in cool water
use whatever self-care
you'd teach your daughter
when she is hurting
because emotional wounds
need to be treated
too

-to my readers

www.ingramcontent.com/pod-product-compliance
Lightning Source LLC
Chambersburg PA
CBHW061326040426
42444CB00011B/2795